The Rise
After
The Fall

Richard D France

First published in Great Britain in 2016 by DeafNoise
Foundation

A CIP catalogue record for this title is available from the
British Library.

The publishers would like to thank Stacey Communications
for their help and assistance in the publication of this book.

ISBN 978-1-5272-0423-2

Cover Art by Mark Bushell
Printed and bound by Book Printing UK, Peterborough, UK.

DeafNoise Foundation
DeafNoiseUK
No: 159
2 London Bridge Walk
London SE1 2SX

E: deafnoiseuk@gmail.com

CONTENTS

To DB
Of the USSR

You are the Angel of Light
Renewing my faith in Life
You flew away with a flutter
And left me with a smile.

INTRODUCTION

Leaving behind the rigid confines of my hospital bed at King's College Hospital, London, I was transferred by ambulance to the Bluebell Ward at Springfield Hospital in Tooting. I was glad to leave but filled with trepidation knowing my next move was to be transferred to a psychiatric hospital. Except this one was going to be different to all the other psychiatric units I had been in as it was primarily for deaf patients. I had no idea what to expect but prepared myself mentally for the potential violence I would face as was the norm in previous stays in mainstream psychiatric hospitals. This time though it would be different, perhaps more difficult, because I was now confined to a wheelchair. I still had no idea if I would be able to walk, whether I would be able to stand and shave in front of a bathroom mirror and wondered if this was it, a life in a wheelchair.

There was a lot of internal strife going on inside my mind. A persistent torment that had had risen from my fated jump into the River Thames. The consequences of an irrational mind that decided going into an unknown void was a far better choice than to persist with the mantra of everyday mundane life. It wasn't making much sense right now considering the damage I had inflicted upon myself. What would the future now hold for me? Would I still lose everything I desired to lose anyway? There was no logic to this self-inflicted process and only now as the ambulance drove through Tooting Bec towards a leafy paradise of old historical buildings with lush greenness that would become my home for the next eleven weeks.

The Rise After The Fall, follows my journey while I was receiving treating at the Bluebell Ward, chronicling my thoughts during my stay there. Perhaps it is a cathartic journey I have to make in order to understand myself better, to try wrestle back control from these demons in my mind. To try conquering this restlessness that has so far led to nine suicide attempts. To try to understand why I am so self-destructive. Perhaps this is my last chance to redeem myself and make the best I can of my situation even if it meant a lifetime in a wheelchair.

Suddenly the ambulance pulled to a stop and I was wheeled out towards a lift, realising that the Bluebell Ward was situated upstairs. I was very hesitant and reluctant to go in but I had no choice because the ambulance crew were in charge of my wheelchair. Control was taken out of my hands and placed into theirs so perhaps this is fate intervening, taking control of my foolishness, of my irrationalism and my persistent death wish.

I was wheeled along a corridor upstairs towards a locked door by the nursing team of Bluebell Ward, who were signing away in British Sign Language. How strange to be taken to a place where language is of the flapping hands choice. On entering the ward, I prepared for the first sound of violence, torment and disagreement but finding only silence as met the other patients for the first time. This was spookily eerie. Where was the ritual of welcome that I had experienced in mainstream psychiatric units? Who was the leader of the ward? How long would it be before the next bout of violence erupted? But there was nothing but politeness and professionalism with the nursing team welcoming me using sign language with open body language and facial expressions. The other patients also made me feel welcome, greeting me, offering tea and biscuits, asking the usual direct and forthright questions that only the deaf community truly understands.

I was shown to my room which was the disabled bedroom on account of my physical disabilities and the space I needed for my wheelchair. My room overlooked the lush gardens of the hospital grounds with the sun's rays shining through. A flock of parakeets skimmed by the window and the trees lulled gently in the late morning breeze. I felt so uneasy as everything was just so quiet, so friendly and welcoming. Was this a trick? An illusion? Will the horrors of my past experiences soon follow? I was shown around the ward and before I knew it, it was lunchtime where I was wheeled towards the dining room. How very strange – so many thoughts were racing through my mind. Everyone is a patient yet seemingly "normal" in comparison to my previous experiences. I noticed the cutlery made of metal yet there was no sense of any threats. I saw people queuing for lunch in an orderly fashion and sitting simply, and ready to eat. It was so, so quiet. Surely, something would kick off soon?

The journey from King's College Hospital to the Bluebell Ward took its toll on my recovering spine as this was the longest period of time I had been sat upright. I went to lie down in what would be my sanctuary and slowly the afternoon sun passed over my eyes as I drifted to sleep to forget the pain. It was a strange experience to suddenly have this freedom and independence after being under twenty four hour observations at King's College Hospital. For sure this ward was locked and I was in a wheelchair, but I could freely come and go around the ward. I could make myself a cup of tea if I so desired. All the nursing team on duty came and introduced themselves using sign language. I was feeling strange when it occurred to me that I was feeling assured, feeling the crumbs of comfort, feeling safe and at ease. There was no violence that day.

The next morning, I wheeled myself out of my room and was promptly greeted a pleasant good morning by a nurse, again in sign language. I quickly had to go back into my room, shut the door and then come out again with a sense of unease. Yet there he was, still signing away to me and informing me of my breakfast choices, all in sign language. There was a quiet hustle and bustle on the ward, of other patients getting up, getting showered and getting dressed ready for breakfast. On my first night, I had even left my hearing aid in overnight to ensure that I would be alerted to any sounds or disturbance yet all I heard was the absolute pure silence – for me it was simply strange as all these thoughts raced through my mind. There was no shouting, no screaming and no banging. Just utter unbelievable peace.

I met the psychiatric team who would be looking after me and again, they all communicated in sign language. It was so surreal for me to meet such professionals, such mental health experts that could communicate in such a beautiful language that immediately put me at ease. And it was at this very moment that I cried and cried for the first time since my jump. I cried because I couldn't believe I had wanted to die. I cried because I had seriously damaged myself. The team reassured me and informed me that it would take some time but they were confident that their treatment and their work with me would heal me, enable me to recover and find myself again.

In the eleven weeks I stayed at Bluebell Ward, my mind went through so many conflicting emotions. Anguish, sorrow, pain, hate, tenderness, love and acceptance. I really can't thank the staff enough for their time in healing me, but not only that, I have to thank the patients too. They were the ones who made me feel 'normal', despite their own issues. There were moments of happiness and sadness but always acceptance. A sense of belonging and equality.

Towards the latter weeks, I became fraught at the thought of returning to society, returning to work. During all this time, I had Cognitive Analysis Therapy, which really changed the way I viewed myself and enabled me to accept myself. The sessions I had with Dr H really inspired me to renew my desire to rejoin society. The physiotherapy sessions enabled me to learn how to walk once again. The nursing staff were always there for me and very attentive too. Without these people, I would have never made it to where I am today. To those people, I thank you all.

In the end, I was keen to leave. Perhaps familiarity really does breed contempt but it wasn't that. I was ready to face the world and return to my life, to the unknown challenges that lie ahead. I had already returned to my job using my crutches to hobble onto the tube at Tooting Bec and travel all the way to Warren Street. I learnt how to wobble everywhere I went struggling with the escalators and stairs as well as bemusing my employers whilst doing my daily ritual of exercises on the office floor during lunch breaks.

Soon the time came to leave and while I was thankful for this opportunity to rejoin the rat-race of England, to join the masses of London, to sample the delights of being free once again, I was sad to leave behind such wonderful people, the medical team and all the patients. Life is a continuous journey and we must make the best of every moment while we breathe.

This book, The Rise After The Fall, chronicles all my thoughts while on Bluebell Ward. It was cathartic for me as I was sober, clean and free from any undue influences. I had a brand new mind, a new way of understanding myself and an eagerness to get back to contributing my part to everyday society and to life. London wasn't ready just yet to reject my contribution. London was always there and always calling me back into her delightful teases. What a city and the city that enabled me to find myself again and renew my connections with life once more. I only had one chance and this time, I wasn't going to waste it. Life is beautiful but it comes in many colours and disguises. My mind was remapped but the persistent thoughts will always be with me. It challenges me every day while I seek the meaning of life. I meet new people who offer their perspectives on what life is all about and continue to do so. I continue to learn and listen, to weigh up and think through, to seek advice and guidance.

Once again, thank you to all those at Bluebell Ward because you really did rock my world back to life. I am no longer the Fallen Icarus, but the Phoenix. I shall rise after the fall.

To the special sardine who came into my life and filled me with sunshine.
With your eyes and love of the sun, I was able to write these words with conviction.
Your mind knows darkness like mine and you allowed me to breath.

You renewed something in me I cannot explain yet I will always enjoy afternoon tea with you wherever we go.

Forever your heart will shine in me.

ONE

Doubt Alone

I am here without a doubt
To find the true self within
However as time passes by
I am continuously alone
Am I repulsive to others
Or do I merely reject me
It is hard to fathom
That aside from siblings
There is nobody but only me
I find this tough to handle
For alone I can carry
But surely there is more
To life than isolation
At this age in which
To reflect and momentarily pause
I seek and gain nothing
Surely my own shadow
Would want to spend time
With me for company's sake
But as the sun goes down
And shadows turn into night
I find defining myself
Through others who make me
Feel I have a purpose, an aim
But I am bereft of such people
I am alone and totally alone
A sense of uneasiness falls
To accept that I will be alone.

TWO

Vacant Eyes

To lead by idly as I lie in thought
A travesty in accepting this ill-ease
I cannot seem to rest nor easily accept
That there is nothing but self to absorb
Surely for all that has been sacrificed
It's hardly a wonder that I indulge
Seeking purpose without redemption
For nothing else can be sought
Within deepness must come to accept
That the only friend long lost paws
And after that only purpose in work
Soon the denial began to outlash nought
In this four stated confined mentally
While rounded in groove achieve zero
Am trying for a lifetime reminder
Waiting for the realness of something
However all seems somewhat repulsed
Nobody except in a virtual world
Just empty space and a lost reason
Here to learn to walk proud once again
Today is only the first of a full day
Already falling towards doom
Ejecting the self to seek sanctuary
Finding nothing but of the same
There has to be a reason for all
Otherwise again I find my ghosts
A past tormented with pain
Open eyes and a furrowed mind.

THREE

This Seeping Madness

Madness is prevalent
It is everywhere
Only today it's well hidden
For we'd go insane otherwise
All these Doctors and Nurses
Who work all hours to save us
We the barking nonsense mad
Who wish to roam the streets fully
It is a tough life being insane
You can't fill in an application form
The shops don't stock on it either
It's imposed through misfortune
A path littered with blemishes
No-one knows where it comes from
Nor have witness to its birth done
There is nothing quite like madness
A sense of futile sorrow
Followed by trigger happy smiles
We the those who are inflicted
Take no pride in this imposed weight
It takes more than strength
To open lead-ridden eyes
We the those who are inflicted
Find no joy in living this way
What are we to do but strive
The best for another tomorrow to come
We the those who are inflicted
We the those who are barking insane.

FOUR

The Friday Of Bliss

Oh not another Friday night
Of the fifth week to sojourn
I long to sit on our settee
And share those saucy kisses with her
Let those who come to condemn
Fill their ears and eyes with denial
For this is what we truly feel
Without words bidden to describe
We simply melt into the night
A touching of fleshy delight
Not going overboard with mirth
Just simply enjoying tonight
How I long to sit beside her
To sense her warmness and delight
For she is true to herself with me
And I sink into her starry eyes
A touching of wondrous hair
Shivers down the spine supine
Time exists for a nothingness
We just sink deeper into pleasure
What a wonder she is to me
Only becomes harder to reach
Oh not another Friday night
Of the fifth week to sojourn
Life is for the living to love
Condemn life at your peril
For she is life and walks life
Such a pearly Queen delight.

FIVE

Fraught

Here I sit
Thinking just how
It came to be
High and low
A travesty of the mind
Life simplified
Transaction of the heart
Sorrow in the learning
Another life ended
Only this morning
I wake to sense
That perhaps today
Will be a different day
High and low
Nobody knows
Which way I'll go
Be warned to
Be aware
Of the danger signs
Only last time
I never knew
Just how far I'd go
High and low
What a crow
To carry when I wake
Simplified
High and low
Watch the danger signs.

SIX

This Blossoming Spring

Today
A day of cloud
Begrudging sun
Never contempted
A light
Comes to visit
Voices recant
Soon in the outdoors
Dancing with the wind
Hair billows
Bristles free
To see the tree
Come soon to blossom
A late seasoning
Yet it comes
Yellow fields
Shimmering green
Soon the tarmac
Returns to
The wooden door
And the light
Will be gone
But behind
Left a smiling face
After all
We are connected
Time by time
Joy will return.

SEVEN

Shimmering Summer

The first
Day
Of summer
Upon us
Like a
Billowing
Breeze
Brings warmth
And
Radiance
In which we
Delight
Waking so
Late
Tales of haste
And we
Forgot to
Say our prayers
Of thanks
To the
Cosmics
For soon we
Shall be
Outside on
The
Slumbering breeze
Eating
Ice cream.

EIGHT

Wisecrack

Wisecracks are easily misunderstood
And in the wronged ear lead to misadventures
For those who take death defying leaps
The consequences are very deadly
Now that the wheels are in motion
A slow return to a sense of normality
We seek them and those everywhere
The they who carry the moral fibre
Sometimes they really don't understand
That a true Englander has humour
Only it seems that mine is too dark
I carry mirth and dish it out
Like plentiful confetti at an endless wedding
All I want is cheer in a grey nation
But dour is essential at times it seems
Nobody but life knows hypocrites
Encouraging us to trip up to oblivion
As soon as you sideline the conventional
They come scurrying looking for entrapment
Cameras and radio mikes in their suitcase
A paranoid nation that cannot laugh
What is this if we cannot blacken humour
Only behind closed doors they insist
Onwards and upwards for the privileged
But for the downstairs people be warned
They built the walls so high
Your sights become blind to all
So be sure to keep secretly laughing.

NINE

Dogma Mantra

And again another Sunday comes to pass
The first of Summer's twilight mindset
We screech mentally yet groan apathetically
Waiting for the day to come when we sojourn
A denial of the tomorrow yet to come at dawn
When all will raise cacophony in the alarming
Then jolt into motion for we are no longer carefree
We turbo towards a dancing to rise
Challenges of the week ahead dogmatically imposed
I cannot fanthom any denial of this reality
For life is such a beautiful entity to deny
From clockface to digital presentation
We all carry the mode of historical production
For somewhere lies someone licking the cream
And at the bottom the inspirer dreams
Onwards we motion for we believe in dreams
And nobody knows what the truth of tomorrow will be
Cranky already on the precipice of tomorrow
Yet this beautiful first day of Summer isn't done
For twilight is delighted to be delayed
So that the birds and the bees can motion
Knocking on our putrid mindset of Winter
To highlight eyebrows observing this new Spring
And today is such a beautiful day to waste
To be thinking that nonsense is comical
For everyone in this life has an unrevealed reason
For tomorrow has yet to happen in disgrace
For tonight we shall listen to the last of the skylarks.

TEN

From That To This

Another damned lie for this is Monday
We delude ourselves that this is the beginning
Dishing out the ideas of plentiful monies
Only those with the knack and poison win
Five long days ahead for the conventional
Dogmatic robots who know no other way
Just the weekend to look forward to
Then life for them becomes very meaningful
We're all on the slippery slope to oblivion
Nowhere to sense but a purpose to strive for
For with losing reason we will grind still
A roof over our heads is a vital motivator
Having forgotten that many years ago outside
We lived and hunted beasts to eat
Squealing throat cutters and nothing to waste
And now here we have the machines to serve
Soon we'll be redundant television squawkers
Mind without logic and permanent shopping channels
Hence we must work to earn so we can spend
It is only Monday but a bargain to be had
Drones dogmatic syndrome nonplussed surplus
We have no reason except for the few
Those who question the system get kicked
However all is not lost as the equilibrium restored
No-one fucks the system and wins against it
Foolproof having hundreds of years to perfect
For now get that head thinking back on track
It's only Monday and someone wants your profit.

ELEVEN

Domestic Queen

She's there in her marigolds
A Divine in the sounding
All accord to domestics
Housebound with flowers
She's always at home
In her satisfied kitchen
A pleasure that no man can give
And she smiles with delight
Flowers get old with time
And she fills another jar
Lifegiving water and vitality
Her neck itches with a longing
For something sweet and soft
And another brush through her hands
She deeply thinks of stolen kisses
While listening to her music
That makes her hips to dance
Kitchen domestics forever
A paradise in her heart
Cleanliness a must
While chaos of the world spins
Marigolds always on the move
Gleaming and bacteria free
She's longing for something
Stubbornly independent
Lovingly beautiful
A kitchen domestic goddess
Damn so good to see.

TWELVE

Plague On The Brain

This is the third of the sixth
A slow decline of acceptance
Having to dig out the soul
To find the destructive blues
On this condemned mind ward
Seeking my own sanctuary
Will I ever be free of demons
That plague me everyday
Those that come with words
Encourage to fight for the truth
Just sometimes there are dark days
And the Doctor with a pill bag
Lurks furtively in the background
I know what needs to be done
Just as what was with the physical
Now to be done with the mental
Time really has no meaning
Just a senseless deconstruct
Looking for love within
To destruct the self loathing
Acceptance of the true norm
I can be and shall become
Destiny always teasing ahead
So plough on foot soldier
End the battle of your soul
The trueness will shine
And love shall come a-calling
Foot soldier find your heart.

THIRTEEN

Choice

The drums are beating
My heart is slowing
Breathing on a motion
Hesitation awaiting
This path is mine
Nor others to choose
A darkness surrounds
Morose morbidity
Only here could it
Be freely spoken
Brethrens amongst us
Death wish mob
We avoid the stares
Hidden conversations
Beachy Head mentioned
A fall too far
Life is the living
Category in choosing
Everyday at a time
Passing clouds again
Will it ever end
Sorrow of the mind
A darkness seeps
Sweeping sickness
Only amongst the brethren
Do we understand
Don't need no Doctor
Just my own choosing.

FOURTEEN

Awakening

Life is the vitality
A cog in the everyday
I am no machine
Defunct humanoid defect
Of every dawn's rising
Eyes shall come to observe
For this is the one path
Destiny in its calling
While the crows are cawing
And trees shimmer blossom
The Spring in us all
Of joy in awakening
While fending off the blues
Sorrow has no place today
For mirth is compulsory
Now is the passing
Of the day's woes indeed
Blue skies on the breeze
And turmoil on the streets
Everyday in motion
A stunning retrospective
Brightness not always reflective
For this is the house of crazy
And we owe the true people
Amongst the categorised
Hidden in your density
Pavement motion blues
We have dancing feet.

FIFTEEN

Hope Revival

Of this enchanted evening
I feel a glimmer of light
Perhaps destiny has come to tease
To remind us of life's vitality
There is a reason for my living
An ultimate purpose of tomorrow
No matter the darkness
From all those yesterdays
We must strive to live
With positivity and observation
An acute eye for details
Ensuring that the flag flies
Pessimism can be converted
But not necessarily all negative
Onwards to strive alive
For the eternal optimism burns
Life is for the living
Even in days of dark
Crutch underneath this Gaia
For the rotation askew
We have our purpose each
From birth to the end
It is the inbetween
That really matters
Remember the sunshine
How it awaits the moon
Eternal stars shining
Brings a grin to this life.

SIXTEEN

Desperation Hues

The beating of the drums
Come closer as you run
A darkness in firelight
And soon everything burns
Run for lives at mercy
Of the unknown shadow
There will be no return
For once death has visited
Renewal in desperation
A sense of flight
The past always carries pain
Whereas all the tomorrows are unknown
The booming of the drums
Always ringing in your head
Nowhere to flee but must run
Soon comes rebirth in safety
And everything begins to renew
What was it of the night
That spewed fire and violence
A mind shook up in fervour
Paranoia tastes bittersweet
Was it all just a dream
Or am I caged in this mind
Longing to break free
Only constrained by time
Move an itch to gain a mile
And soon this burden will be free
The booming of the drums.

SEVENTEEN

Invasion

Interlopers
Of the mind
They intrude
When not
Wanted
Thinking
They know all
But really
They
Are nothing
Otherwise
They wouldn't
Be
Interlopers
They do
Not
Realise I have
Fire and light
Life
Alive
Burning
In my eyes
Interlopers
Intruders
Pests on the
Ward
Interlopers
Terminated.

EIGHTEEN

This Passing Day

Of the sixth on the six
All eyes on the outcast
Hovering clouds hesitate
While times manifest
Awaiting for the heave
Outbound towards trees
Replenish oxygen
While gabbering free
Finally they arrive
Hungry and filled with pee
Expurge and exhale
They sit to tell tales
Soon we are out
Out there free again
In the big machine
On four trundled round
Outbound towards trees
Longing for escape
Only knowing to return
We rejoice at this air
People around roam
A joy in being free
Wheeled around in glee
Mud on the clean treads
Soon to return bound
And a bed to lie in rest
A day of gladdening
Dreams soon to return.

NINETEEN

Goodbye Again

Of a thwarted tale
That was diverted
By a great leap
Everything changed
A longing desire
In the need to live
Re-evaluate
Reconsiderate
Those to have loved
Those to say goodbye
Forever in my heart
Anguish no more
This heart burns
A bright flame
For you within
A desire constrained
Cannot unleash
Sudden impulse
Gently simmer
For love flows
People around
Always in mind
Longing to strive
Forever free
The sun shines
Clouds bring rain
Let's dance tonight
For tomorrow will come.

TWENTY

Insanity Breeds

Is this life on a reset
Where everything introspected
A harshness under glare
The all-seeing Doctor's eye
Outside the tree's blossom
Life simmers with its brine
Peopled by the ignorant
We the crazies holed up
Under control of the doctrine
No escape without permission
Not a shit with observation
Will this journey endure
Or does self discovery pursue
An awakening of values
To accept life as a prize
Nobody except the self
Can muster this energy
Onwards as time travails
A transversing of the path
No more cloudy days
For this sun is instilled
All causes ignored
For symptoms observed
The longing shall return
And towards the lively path
Let feet mortal shuffle
For old age is the only grace
Onwards towards life.

TWENTY ONE

Lost In Love's Dream

Will she wake in time to catch this golden dawn
Or does she slumber through dreams reaching out to
Grandma
Will the afternoon jasmine scented breeze catch her breath
Does Bobbi hope for another bedsheet pee
Is breakfast going to be another lollipop
Or will chicken come to roost in a hot oven
Might she find the splendour in her walk
Or will the steaming iron calk to her standing soaked
Does she loll in her delicate pyjamas
Twitching her golden smile at tomorrow's unbidden horse
Will she think of him again today
Or is the Russian harshly dismissive awake
Will Sunday be her day to enjoy despite the trailing ex
Does she laugh at his jokes
Cinematic times inbetween her boys and popcorn
Let this Easter Sunday bring her joy
Perhaps in time yet to tick will come a kiss
Or is resistance futile in the knowing heart
Tick tock will only reveal
Whether Cupid has struck its arrow in our hearts
A destiny yet to be revealed and with mirth
Enjoy the day's unravelling
To you that makes me sing with joy
And for crazy days that follow bringth safety
For there is nothing but assurance
While despite the woes we continue to blossom
Words just for you from every heartbeat
To you and only you forever.

TWENTY TWO

Restless

The first of the seventh is here
A long vapour trail of the mind
Longing to beat my trap in the sun
A bank holiday brings lazy staff
Swarmed with ward incidences
In which tea is the highlight
There is escapism in us all
Longing to forget this dogma
Isn't life just a beautiful
No need for further descriptions
Just plain old eternal life
And from here we motion forward
Cheering whenever the Queen appears
Ain't no hallucination
For headless souls manifest
A history of seepages
And we can only look back
To think of long cold hard days
Lost in the furrow of tomorrows
What will be will bring
Just remember reality from fantasy
Then plough headfirst into nothing
For then your footsteps create
A future from long lost dreams
Longing for hot summer days
A bank holiday on the ward
Tick tock is the impatient clock
Seek the sanctuary of your mind.

TWENTY THREE

Murmur Of A Heartbeat

The surprise of the sun
A shadow in the door
Slumber in the sweetness
She carries a heart
Such feelings soar
Upwards and above
Higher than a cloud
Out below the sun
Her eyes filled
Yearning replenish
To know delight
In language mirth
Two become one
A sense of belonging
Home is the feeling
Of knowing to join
She carries a heart
Everything matters
Nothing hesitates
Continue this path
For it leads to
What you yearn
Laidback in plush
No need for cushions
Trueness lies beyond
And all else matters not
For it is true what they say
She carries a heart.

Manifesto Dogma

I am
The manifesto
Doctrination
Machination
Terminal applause
The disease
Is
In you
And you
Have
No way of
Knowing
How
We know
Your
Intentions
I is
The we
And we
The I
Machine
Indoctrination
Manifesto
Hesitation
Terminal bleeding
And soon
To come
Your termination.

TWENTY FIVE

Realisation

In the synopsis of life
A short cut curtailed
There is no easy way
Except to endure pain
For every step you take
There is a motion surge
Bound forward keep looking
A crossroad no hesitation
Directions are nought in this
For destiny will carry you
A wind billows as you walk
Glimmering stars beckon
Follow your instincts
Nobody but only you knows
See where the ripples shine
On the ever floating sea
You'll know when you arrive
Peopled by familiar strangers
Just love is all you need
Then bound home you'll know
Keep rocking your rhythm
There's no music except your mind
An applause for nothing
Freely given and gratefully received
Just remember the old
With their wise words of ghosts
Your past is what makes you
But the future defines your today.

TWENTY SIX

Unease

Of wireless
No birds on a remote
Increased transmission
Oppressive silence
Nature in retreat
We compound in advance
All must not resist
Futility in ignorance
Radiation dosage
Cutting back on cancer
Replaced with drones
A mindset lost
We know all
But you have nought
There is nothing to do
Except entertain
Nobody can escape
This is the new truth
Continue to obey
For we carry keys
A loss is yours only
Gain ours to take
We are the masters
And you shall serve
Continue to entertain
You have nothing
Only drivel to offer
Continue to manifest.

TWENTY SEVEN

Scorched Eyes

Shifting sands are not a necessity
When implanted feet of trust is all
No need to furtively lurk in shadows
When truth is easily outspoken free
An optional choice is what you have
While incarnated I remain inside
Just remember where you are standing
While the hoardes roam over my head
An appreciation of all as you sought
Doesn't diminish my worthiness in all
I am the freedom personified
When others seek to impose on
Love is a truly lovely trait
But I cannot go home no more
Life is what continues when peril strikes
But recovery follows in pain as a desire
This mind burns brightly as a fire
Scorching all that closely shim too
And feathers were just the illusion
Tenderness is for those I truly love
And that includes you but bearably
Remember I too am human trait
And not fallible failure featured
I shall return and to shine my light
Nobody will crimson my path no more
For this is my destiny calling so near
See with blinded eyes for senses sparkle
Remember I too am human trait.

TWENTY EIGHT

A Wander In The Night

Her laughter ripples across the scented lake
As trees bend to hear her voice
Soon comes a splash and another
Lovers swimming in the moonlit water
Without a care but for each other
Eyes shimmering with love
Holding gently and caressing sweetly
A racing heart swirling with passion
Soon lips come to greet and dance
All night long on this summer twilight
Nobody but themselves to enjoy pleasures
With only the stars and moon to witness
A simmering fire of passionate woes
Love is here to stay and rein towards old age
Will you be my forever?

TWENTY NINE

Sense Of Nothing

The ripples of life
Extend beyond safe
Just when you think
All is settled
A pebble dropped
And equilibrium upset
Essential to change
No more dependency
Only own feet
To stand tall and proud
Look inwards to seek
A gathering of wits
In denial of life
A habit of long
Pull out the shade
Instil with light
Does it really matter
For only those
Who make contact
Are the ones
That really matter
Even if nobody does
Then it's all
Down to you
To make of life
How it should be
Heads up high
Keep smiling freely.

THIRTY

Corrode

I am
Sorry invincible
Corroded
Aggregated
Core of soul
Destruction
Timeless suffering
Turned
To
A beauty of
Life
Living life's joy
Sorry invincible
Corroded
Segregated
Separation
Of the mind
Entwined soul
Singing
Nonchalance
Chanting
Ain't no
Lisping
In this state
Of the mind's
Sorry invincible.

THIRTY ONE

Passing Days

Oh such wonderous feelings
That leaves one soaring high
Longing to return to life
When this world's a-turning
Days like this are blipping
A shortness stretched long
How the desire to return
To the maddening crowds looms
Life is a wonderful feeling
Although the lows can be harsh
In this cavern of mindless
A senseless passing of day
Soon the reality hits again
Legs that cannot go places
A healing is a journey
Delving deep within inside
No more wonderings
Just this barren truth
Defining oneself through others
A longing to want to identify
The day is a-passing
And gripping while losing
Wanting to go back to norm
But the history is now no more
At least the longing is to live
In desperation to thrive
Home is where the heart sings
Be true to oneself pride.

THIRTY TWO

Void

I am
The
Self sabotage
Invincible
Indestructible
Self sorrow
Harrowing
Mental anguish
Tormented
In pain
To ease
I become
The
Self sabotage
Sorrow invincible
An uneasiness
In seeking
The
Self destruction
For reason
Not known as
To why
But
Persistence
Without doctors
Is a
Harrowing
Experience.

THIRTY THREE

Futility

This is the Sunday
Perpetual precipice
Hesitation doubtful
A wandering mind
The sun falters
Comes no rain
Of this mood
Lost in shade
Glimmering eyes
Outlook forecast
A head for nowt
While wrestling time
Longing to go
To break free
Healing time is hard
Everything goes slow
Only the maniacs
Go full speed ahead
Soon for them
Comes the headcrash
We must falter
For a thinking mind
Can be dangerous
When it collides
With the physical
Tough healing times
A lost mind
Another dawn passes.

THIRTY FOUR

Roaming Nowhere

What am I if I am to define myself
By surroundings I linger in
Does this make me live at the forefront
Of this exciting plentiful life's frontiers
When through nothingness I cannot define
Except to be a self based on nothing
But ideas that come from thoughts
Right now my four walled cube
Comes to define my existence
Into a 3-D dimension of unworthiness
And yet I cringe from such thoughts
For I know life is far more beautiful
Only I know the confine of my existence
In my wheelchair to which I cannot
Roam freely as expected due to inclines
Of this Tooting that I have yet
To explore and enjoy for every step
Isn't a step forward but a hurdle
And in my stubborn independent streak
I cannot abide by the rules of others
For whom help is a necessity and to
What I cannot gladly receive
For this attitude only foils my positivity
And I remain stuck in this 3-D parallel
Of my own misfortune and making
Only by uplifting and creative thinking
Can I expect to think out of the box
And tomorrow will bring me hope.

THIRTY FIVE

Out Of Choices

Hear the drums that beat internally
A heartbeat on the unison motion
Eyes that glimmer filled with hopes
And passion once again simmers
There are the two differences
Of choices to be offered and made
One so sweet and tempestuous
And another easily laidback
Of choice that baffles with life
Decisions do not need to be made
Kissing is the infinitival affirmation
A delight in the gathering heart
How is it such choices came to fruit
With this delight of life's choosing
Plumb and ripe in the tasting
Although one of only urging
What is love if we cannot define
What are choices if decision cannot choose
Another leaving of one's heart
But the path continues to weave
No affirmation to be made
Only another prescription for Viagra
She knows who she is
She knows what she has
She knows of the choices
In banishing a strangeness
Of this path that meanders
Onwards to fickle decide for love.

THIRTY SIX

Filth Savage

Lax is the suggestive bile
In which treason in the everyday
A terminal in the unknown
For reason beyond doubt
This is the dogma of the week
A turmoil in upheaval
We know time stretches
Yet with blindness we avail
All the unbidden tomorrows
Of thoughts that corrode
Beyond our knowing
We prevail senselessly
Oh mighty weather
Bring me clouds of doubt
Oh mighty rain
Wash away this filth
Life the entity thrives
Yet this sorrowed doom
Onwards with another
One by one we plunder
Slicing time with purpose
While age travails skin
Is this our reasoning
To economic slaves
Plunder all with lies
For true reason knows
Beyond doubt lies hesitation
Don't falter in every step.

THIRTY SEVEN

Manana

Come the days when the future arrives
A longing in the tensed held
Tomorrow cannot be here until dawn
For today is the day of beckoning
No room for soiled minds
For others come to contaminate
A longing of wanting to break free
But stuck in the confines of hold
These are just the four walls
Only a perception that restrains
Life is a beautiful entity
Just remember the destiny
If it seems so long and far
It's only because your heart must beat
There's no need to run
When joy's in the pleasure of stillness
We all strive to achieve dreams
A longing for freedom pleasures
Grass remains green as skies blue
Just a mood and state of mind
Longing to freedom stroll
For this path has many years
Onwards with embolden
Forward to all the futures
Persistence is no false trait
Only a belief is all required
Onwards will never a path cold
For the sun shall always rise.

THIRTY EIGHT

The Love Of Electric

This is
The
Time of
Evolution
Where
Electricity
Crackles
Its own
Cackle
Knowing
We
Are
Dependent
On this
Filthy
Need
For we
Cannot
Seem to
Leave it
Alone
But to
Atone
By buying
More
And more
Yet our greed
Is never ending.

THIRTY NINE

Simmer Down London

Oooh oooh yeah
Ooooh ooooh yeah yeah
Yeah yeah yeah
Yeahhhh

Gonna be a day
When I feel loving
Ain't no matter where
Cos love is all around

Way down Soho way
Up in Mayfair
Whether you're rich or poor
Love is all around

East is East
West is West
No matter where you go
Gonna share this loving feeling

Trampling across the Strand
Kisses on the Piccadilly
Swooning down Southbank
Loving in this crazy town

Come on come and dance
Get your dancing feet grooving
Ain't no matter where
Cos love is all around.

FORTY

Hesitate

Cometh the hour of eleven
When all small and sought in slumber
A scattering of broken words
And soon the broth spill over to love
In those eyes of yours I seek
A peace that we both yearn for
Lifelong loving without hesitation
In which you can breathe freely oh
While truly being your true self
I long for the comfort of love
Yet my falter is there to hear
For something of you makes me pause
While the sun shines down the Mediterranean
It's all about being truly honest
For broken integrity serves no purpose
Words that spoken and signed are free
But a true heart yearns for more
You are the one that pulls my gravity
Slingshot trajectory on the conscious
Seeking a belonging for life somehow
And you just blow me away constantly
I struggle with your wind of changes
For shifting sands I cannot stand on
A senseless belonging that has no rationale
In wanting to belong with a true heart
Will you ever be the one to open up
Or will your values block this true love
Ease into this groove or be gone.

FORTY ONE

Age Ringing The Future

Is this
The land
Of my dreams
Where
Hopes and destinies
Come true
Is it where
I will
Grow old
A wonderland
Of pleasures
And gratification
Perhaps
Who knows
One day
I will
Meet my
True love
In this
Beautiful
Wonderland
I can
Almost taste
My dreams
Ringing true
Hopes and desires
Everlasting dreams
This wonderland.

FORTY TWO

A Free Spirit

Of this day the fourth on the eighth
A mind fleeting light on the wind
Blossoming Spring and a mental clearance
Slowly we come to deconstruct
In revealing that underneath it all
I am a gentleman with a past
And as the sun shines on this afternoon
I gawp and look at my historical landscape
A vast eerie blot that evokes awe
For to have survived as I have lived
I am fortunate to have my wits today
For pleasure has been sought at a pain
Any yet sorrow comes to light in quiet
For now after another bout of self destruction
I can open eyes and slowly look inwards
To banish my own tormented monsters
And listen carefully to the contaminated
For if this personal ladder is to be climbed
Then cleanliness and sobriety is essential
In order to allow the true self to manifest
And slowly it comes out the true of I
For there is no ego but pride in collectivism
A gathering of knowledge and skills
Contributing to this development of soul
The fiery spirit tempered to pleasantness
And for once again let life be reset freely
With all the tomorrows to look forward to
Inside the spiritual and soulful true self.

FORTY THREE

Sweetness Under A Roof

Longing to live so I can breathe
Longing to stand so I can see horizons
Time's a tricky concept of the mind
Days spin fast when everything's slow
We long to roam free but must work
For glory days really need paying for
A history of being on the perpetual move
Looking for a place I can call home
Only a room to put in my beloved bed
And a senseless window with a view
May the sun shine in the mind everyday
Might the path at night come with the moon
Life is a timeless path until destiny is found
No wondering can ever achieve the future
Myths are perpetuated on the silver screen
Grim reality is just a dustcloth away
Shine as you should for you are beautiful
Stop this doubting mind causing plague
Look up to the sky whenever feeling low
Thinking of the music waiting to be created
Longing to urge forward with solid feet
Keep moving with the joy of life's glee
Onwards is the only omnipotent in you
For everyday is a brand new day of joy
Linger only if it beautifies your mind
Cast aside those doubts and live no lies
Onwards with the music of gorgeous life
Forever in the shadow of the universe.

FORTY FOUR

Longing Lost

Let sorrow dissipate
Allow love to blossom
A growth in the heart
For tenderness shall thrive
We know nothing
Of the tomorrows
To come
Yet everyday feels
Such a blessing
That we must dance
While there is music
Love is a joy
As our path lies ahead
Destiny calling us home
We must sorrow
But we will not
Allow it to bear us down
Sunshine smiles
And dances in the rain
A joy to know
That living is good
There'll always be clouds
But nobody can ever
Take away your smile
Those eyes oh yes those eyes
I want to dance in them
Those eyes oh yes those eyes
Filled with tender love.

FORTY FIVE

Ego Mantra

I
Am the
Indestructible
Persona
Invincible
Assailable
Up there
With
The almighty
I
Hold
The power
Of
Light
And Darkness
You
Will all
Bow down
Before
I
Yes
I
The
Indestructible
Persona
Invincible
Assailable
Conqueror.

FORTY SIX

Floating Free

Once again in the fifth of the eighth
Rolls in on the dancing blue clouds
A week that has flown with surprise
The ease in delight of time's passing
To cast eyes on the horizons with flight
A motor to transverse miles of delight
Will time ever let go of this prison
In which a mind becomes stifled still
While wondering of the mirth today brings
Sunny days and passing clouds in glee
And the ink never pauses to think
Moments pass while the seconds tick
Hesitation in the afternoon pause
To be on a bus or sitting tube
Just to feel the delight of life
This modern society we live in
A wonderment of hive and bustle
While others trail home to make love
Cast aside the woes of the week
No more thoughts of bosses on the bile
Dreams filtering off to think of boats
And fields filled with barbequed campers
Onwards and upwards the mind lifts
While in reality physical actuality sits
Not so long before the knowing comes
And soon it shall return to own hands
Life for the living and the pleasure
Cast away over the deep blue seas.

FORTY SEVEN

Roaming

Come and sink with me
For my mind's on a trip
Road to nowhere tonight
But inside we'll fly
Let's go on a trip
Let's ride this current
Skim the breezes high
Hang low under clouds
Come and see inside
Darkness turns to light
A joy in this dreaming
Togetherness we'll bind
Come seek this joy
Come hold my hands
Let's ride so far
Let's go find home
Together we can smile
A joy forever ours
Spirits entwined forever
Sealed with loving hearts
Let's our two join
Be together forever one
Let's ride so far
Let's go find home
Let's go on a trip
Road to our home
Together forever entwined.

FORTY EIGHT

Eighteen Minutes

I've got eighteen minutes
That's all I've been given
Eighteen minutes of loving
And all I wanna do
Is gonna take much longer
In eighteen minutes
I'm gonna express
A lifetime of loving
Eighteen minutes is all
All I'm gonna get
To give to you tonight
They're sending the car round
Men in green suits
The head doctors are coming
With their big nasty needle
So hey come come along
I've only eighteen minutes
To express to you
All I wanna say to you
All I want to express
All my desires for you
Eighteen minutes is all
They're giving me only
Eighteen short minutes
Gonna make it last
A long long lifetime
Eighteen minutes.

FORTY NINE

Tinkling eyes

Suddenly in light's evening beamers
She came as if an angel arrived
With a smile of gold and eyes alive
Hope restored that renewed vigour
Will we ever meet in the shadows
A brethren who thwarts brotherly moves
Siblings of a lifelong acknowledge
And the spirits were out to chase
For with delight she could bring
In the impasse of the two to know
Decisions couldn't allow be imposed
For life is too beautiful to fragment
And suddenly it all fell to reveal
That a heart is still searching more
For settled is the game but none fast
Reality imposed with dogma's game
Breaking the rules of all to dare
Once in love, forever in love
But has the silvery arrow yet to strike
Only time can manifest its truths
And for age to gradually reveal
Oh there's no sense in going home
For the night brings its own pleasures
To not acknowledge is to deny
And once again we must steadfast
For reality is precious to know
Glimmering forever like a diamond mined
Forever to roam til home calls me bid.

FIFTY

Being

Days are returning
A mind on the roam
I long to live
Positive traits
Home will come
Settle to life
Thunderbolt stride
No shame in death
Pride in living
Knowing home is here
Onwards bound
Forwarded motion
Keep striving
Things logic
Music and write
Get out there
Enjoy all
Life is life
Nine times alive
A cat to tell
Dog to inspire
Nature divine
Motion bound
Life is life
Moral and mortal
Sleep and awake
Forward the path
Underfoot shuffle.

FIFTY ONE

Liberation Days

Sunday is here again
And the week turns
Will it bring me closer
To the liberation dream
Weeks have flown
Of being out of action
How I long
To return to the fray
A realisation
That I needed a cry
Hold back this tide
That overwhelmed
Now things are settled
I can breathe easy
Longing to break free
In my own humble home
Sleeping sweetly gentle
On a mattress of mine
The days are passing
And I rein my hands
Oh to rejoin life
Would be a delight
I must wait though
Longing to buzz free
Tick tock in the mind
A scurry of visual feast
Not be long strangers
Before I join your glee.

FIFTY TWO

Slave To Monday

First of the ninth
A timespan stretched
Horizons ever long
But an ending in sight
Seeking sanctuary
Obliged to obey
Sabotage on the mind
Living as clean
Eager to roam
Creeping with time
Longing to get out
With the masses
Another Monday
Feet still
Wanting to go
Soon time will come
Hurry this pace
Mind is shooting
Body healing
A steadiness
We long to escape
To be free
Even in waged slavery
For now I appreciate
The throng on the tube
Eyes cast ignorance
Beckon people stare
Longing to roam.

FIFTY THREE

Reflections Broken

Days are coming
When the great release arrives
Skies turn blue with air so fresh
The door will become my exit
From here on and beyond
I will redempt to do my best
No more substances abuse
No more self-loathing
No more destruction
Life is all living and engaging
All must be seen in the light
The old rages to be dismantled
For in the realisation of forty five
Such rages have got me nowhere
Now I have an opportunity
To broker and facilitate
A brand new future with dreams
All those years of struggle
Have now brought me to this path
There will be many challenges ahead
There will be further dark days
One has to succumb and pacify
The truth is the open honesty
Enjoy while still breathing
Great Star Nation carries you far
Just open up your horizons
The possibilities at your fingertips
Onwards and back into the affray.

FIFTY FOUR

Aspire

Strength comes in many guises
Even when least expected
The strongest in times of duress
The weakness in hours of need
There is no entity in it
Just a manifest reality
And write fables of this
In desperate times
In our hours of despair
In our forlorn lost
Strength has many values
Be it mental or physical
Overwhelmed by the odds
At the point of defeat
Facing death even
Strength has no personal qualms
Found deep within of reserves
A desperation
A cry for help
Losing faith
It comes
What of those who fail
They do not acknowledge
Strength's unique value
The difference
Between living and death
Strength, within us all.

FIFTY FIVE

Ticking The Tock

Lackadaisical
They mull to mither
Standing on restless feet
Hands in the facebook
Staffing issues priority
They forget who we are
Gossip is their ammunition
Work an enemy
They come to preen in pride
To show off their skills
On the flip side of it all
A life of caring
Watching people wither
We know nothing
According to them
Special needs our label
Expertise is theirs
Twitchy clothes that are bland
Easy to dismiss
Egos to carry afar
Then we're forgotten
When their shift's over
Back home on the sweat
Hesitation in the timing
We're left to fester
Another shift to allocate
Tick tock their mantra
Tick tock our dogma.

FIFTY SIX

Unease

Reality has a habit of kicking
Like the first alarm on a Monday
Dreaded feeling knotted uneasy
A gathering pace towards crashing
It knocks you sideways for a time
Then the motioned path continues
Life is a beautiful precious entity
Comes with its battered candour
A rusted edge that lives at the forefront
Newness regenerates its purpose
At times you feel taking two steps back
A disjarred reality conjoined
Suddenly the blue becomes the grey
Clouds gathered in a sudden storm
These are not new feelings visiting
But old ones that have been away a while
There it is again the uneasy feeling
Senseless in its apparent manifest form
There is no colour to it apart from irony
So far there have been no paintings of it
Today has been a kickback day
When dreams were disjarred into reality
Time ticks slower on such grey grainy days
You know everything will be fine tomorrow
Just that it's a long day to get through today
Yet here comes the new quarter moon
Attached and yet detached from your reality
Soon stars will dance then reality sings again tomorrow.

FIFTY SEVEN

Impatience

Tonight
I sit
On the asp
Of a
Verge
Wondering
If tomorrow
Will
Bring
News of
A Standing
Nature
Tomorrow
Is a
Day to
Think
About later
For I
Must
Get through
The
Night
Tonight
Tomorrow
And
Tonight
There is a
Moon shining.

FIFTY EIGHT

Eye Shut Eyes

Of this day that cast ahead
Into a future by the seaside
Once the sun's gone down
Hands will clasp and swing freely
Eyes drawn into one another
Looking ahead into the future
These golden sunsets will never end
As nor will lovestruck heartbeats
For the walking will come again
And days of pleasure soon come
Followed by nights of writhing together
A long drawn sleep filled with dreams
And reality will soon match those night visions
Come soon for we shall have a future
Just carry an open mind for adventures lie ahead
And under the watchful eye of the moon we shall kiss
Only step by step will we arrive there
Ahh this blossoming love
Yes this blossoming love.

FIFTY NINE

Appreciate

Days of this long bidden hour
Only had to be on this day
A time of the long tick tock
Anxious to know the future
Will the walking come bidden
We strive to know immediately
Then the Doctor was brief
A short abrupt inspection
Declaration is over
And walking season partially open
We'll see what the tomorrow brings
Longing to know distances
A ticking walking machine
Part machine devoid human
Full human with a heart
We bolster to boost mentally
For eternity has yet to strike me down
Onwards with the unbidden push
Towards the mysteries of destiny
All will be revealed in time
Only that of the sun and the moon
An edge tempered with the soul
And love's eternal torment
Life is a beautiful entity
Not to be discarded carelessly
We'll see what the new day brings
While the rays of the sunshine beam
And soon to mutt together walk.

SIXTY

Blue Rinse Paradox

Sweet spinster theory
Gotta grow old sometime
Life's a turning forever
Wheels in motion
From candle to grave
A sight and hearing
We never forget ever
Until we go grey
A lifelong memory
It's a wonder
We can remember
All of it yes all
Soon before we know
Life's coming to an end
Blue rinses on a discomfort
Meals for two with a friend
Growing old isn't the end
It's another journey elsewhere
Blue river spinster songs
We carry old stars in our minds
Radio tunes and television
On the repetition renew
Growing is no shame
Just shows we've lived
Friends and family fade
Nobody knows when you'll go
Forever on in the spinster mood.

SIXTY ONE

Letting Go

Is this the true fire that burns me alive
Or am I deluded by the beauty of skin
Knowing what I have tasted of mortal flesh
The knack is in the ability to be at ease
A flare-up for no reason is not a reason
Of love's flammable emotions that pours scorn
Ease and peace should be the aim of the game
A lifelong sense of belonging without rejection
Excuses are always found but uneasiness isn't
Follow the gut's truth and repel all that hurts
Life is a short ride and for dreams to achieve
If she is the one that goes the way of the tide
No matter what the internal desire strives for
For other hearts are more divine in their welcome
She is there standing and waiting for you
Of interests greedily shared and an individual
With the soul of sunshine truly in her heart
No need to combine and mix confusion to reign
It is clear as a day's unfolding dreamy tale
Of a lady from a far flung land easily banished
Just simply cut the ties and seek your truth
You know that of people who repel are noughted
Following the heart of your open road with dreams
There she lies and flesh to succumb devour
Lasting pleasures than to zero restart
Follow your truth and perhaps nothing comes
To know that life is always an everchanging story.

SIXTY TWO

Sensual Movements

Life
Is a
Mover
Whether
You
Like it or not
A river
That
Swims
Without water
Beneath
Your feet
Life
Is a
Dream
That
Becomes true
Whether
You
Are awake or not
Life and dreams
Eyes and ears
Touch and smell
Sensation
Sensual
Is
This incredible
Life.

SIXTY THREE

Labour Blue Hues

Of a day
In which sweat extoils
A realisation that grunt pays
Whether in the factories or machines
For sickness affects those
Subjected to extreme poverty
While in stupor of labour
There can be no stoppage
For the show must go on
And the masses need entertaining
While the sun passes its own shadows
A long to roam free
While time ticks in turmoil
 Wondering if there is any sense
In this madness of slavery
For someone somewhere has a glint
Seeking sanctuary in labour strife
No matter what the weather pours
For clouds are just a passing thought
While wondering what will be sought
Ahh yes money is our ticket
To something beyond salvation
Redeem ourselves in glamour
While drowning in the sins of whoring
And somewhere someone is beheaded
A brutality meted out in the name
And yet we must enslave to work
Money the sin of the world.

SIXTY FOUR

Clock Watcher

Is it the really the ninth week
A stretching of imagination's time
Distance travelled far flung
While uttering with impatience
There is fast and go very slow
Time playing its infinitial tricks
Clocks motioning on the forward
Treason in the mind's senses
Another six weeks in front to go
A timeline that hurts exhaustively
Longing to reign the free roaming
To reclaim once again the streets
Distance is a revelation sprung
Surprises when history created
Memories blur into a seam
Digging for iconic moments
Ticking followed by the tock
Mind games travail with seconds
What's to know how the ahead goes
When looking back leaves surprises
Every singular has its own definition
Bodily time has its pace
We cannot push time faster
We can sleep through it though
Stretching out for a lifetime
Waiting isn't an option for living
Those pavements await my feet
A clean head of no time.

SIXTY FIVE

Seepage Flashback

On the fifth of the ninth
A standing of a new order
The view from high above
Enough to giddy delight
To motion forward huddle
In new world mantra
Seeing the pleasing faces
Delighted to see the walk
In my own heart
Good to motion manifest
Days are still yet young
I have travelled far
Only in mind and body
Now with sticks
I can go further
New aches and pain
Old fears and dreams
All shattered in this
New dogma senses
We haste to forward
A motion in seepage
Not so long ago
A wreckage in the Thames
Now phoenix rising
A bold approach
Life for the living
Appreciation renewed
Onwards towards destiny.

SIXTY SIX

Come To Me

Will she or won't she
A turbulent ripple
In wanting to know
Whether hearts beat or not
For together we burn
And apart repel
Drawn to the light
A dangerous liaison
We don't know
Until we try
Honeypot temptation
Life's cherry pickings
Wanting a terminus
To create that love
Forever entwined
Or to be torn apart
Life in London
Love in London
Bring some peace
To this beating heart
Will she be the one
Or delusion set in
Wanting her heart
Afraid of being hurt
Will she or won't she
Be the one forever
Hearts entwined
Lips to seal.

SIXTY SEVEN

Prison Of This Mind

Can't wait to escape this confine
A mental prison of time
Everything ticks so slowly
While the distance stretches so far
A longing to exit free
Senseless detached belonging
There's an open road out there
Sensing freedom on the air
Roam is the pleasure within
Freedom the name of the game
Tarmac trundles I need
Engines roaring on the accelerate
I long to seek this joy
Of being out there freely
It's only when you're trapped
That appreciation comes truly
Latitude and longitude
Transverses across continents
Only politics of the conventional
Tries to thwart my freedom
You gotta bite your lip with pride
No hesitation in the leaving
Just go for all will be fine
An escaping with your own mind
Cast out in the role
Yes the freedom outcast
Don't allow any prisoners
Just an open mind on the roam.

SIXTY EIGHT

Stolen

They say they are the thwarted revolution
I couldn't believe such inflammatory words
They fought hard and they fought tough
Appreciation of their contribution to the world
Ever since Adam ate Eve's apple it's been wrong
Power stolen from them by masculine brutality
However they are still here and fighting strong
The world's oppression does not stifle them
A dissent in the lifelong fight to equalise
No matter where in the world they dissent
Always brutality meted out to stifle
They always gather to stand and fight
Without weapons but only their voices
Harassing the feeble state powers and armies
Guns and violence usually a reaction
From a mass afraid to give up power
But what they just don't realise is this
Feminity is a force to be reckoned with
Sisterhood of the world unite to equalise
Standing together to oppose this mass suppression
They will not cower even in times of violence
For them masculinity lost the fight
Ever since the power of the gun the world changed
Nobody hesitates to take a life brutally
Standing up to this enforced domination
Sisterhood living up to their true word
What a world we would have without war
Sisterhood standing together in pride.

SIXTY NINE

Heartstring Failure

She's not the one despite your heart singing
Only you want her for all your selfish self
She's a lady who'll go far if she dares
But she can't open her heart to you freely
You gotta be rolling free with your mind
A substance glued to your heart called love
She's a far flung lady that reaches to many
Yet seemingly she's fixated on you for sure
However she does push you away when you get close
Is she really what you want despite your heart
Will you ever rest your weary mind senseless
A loving feeling doesn't carry life forever
If she's the one then why's your heart cheating
A lover of all divine in the Lord's eyes
Treat her right and she'll be yours forever
But she's pushing you away hard and harsh
Is she really the one you wanna grow old with
A lover with her own conventional stiff rules
You know how much you love your freedom
Why can't you find yourself with pleasures
There's a whole big world out there waiting
Ain't no-one you found but yourself sought
She's not the one for you you know in your heart
Is she really what you want for a lifetime
A toil on a broken heart treason'll go round
Is she really the one you give your heart to
You gotta find yourself truly free and happy
Is she the one that will do all your loving?

SEVENTY

Wheelchair Holiday

And it's all go go times again
The tormenting doubts dissipate
A heart's grandeur dream
In a far flung town hustle
We sigh to unwind
Dogs barking for the beach
Rippled waters crashing shoreline
A distant boating captain's pride
Underneath the open blue skies
With an intoxicating sunshine
A billowing comfort breeze
Walks that carry random directions
Onwards towards nowhere
Just a free rein without horse
A loving feeling holding hands
Eyes carrying pearly laughter
To the beaches feet trample
Collapsing on the dunes for love
Cooling naked in the waters
Sitting on a beached trunk
Sandwiches with grit inside
Dogs barking at the waves
Summer days are coming
Get there before the tourists
Ice cream queues meltdown
Our own private beach mat
Longing for this day to live
Forever in heart and mind.

SEVENTY ONE

Stand

This ache
Aching away
Progress comes
Measured in pain
Throbbing like toothache
Back to the chair again
Reluctantly
Want to walk
But this pain
Swollen foot
Aghast at this
The next phase
Pain for six more weeks
Time stretched out
Pain today
For breakfast, lunch and dinner
Supper is just sleep
A pain
Constant
No screaming
Just eat grapes
While trying
Not to think of it
Ouch and ooh
Pain is a measure
Of improving or other
Pain
Ouch.

SEVENTY TWO

Dark Days

And without the crashing release of gates
I yondered to ponder at this sudden reality
Work for the masses piled on an individual
For whom praise from the fat controller sings
Return to the affray and burn your skin
A longing of desirable to habit old
These are ghosts that lie rest to sin
Anew with a fragile mind yet broken
Onwards with acast seas that drift
Sleep only for the weary to give in
Reality comes crashing through siesta
No-one knows the pain of reject
Social outcast on the meandering prowl
No sense of true destiny's path to frown
We listless linger with ringing advice
While in novella terms falsely dream
A longing to go on the open path
Forever to lose these sinful thoughts
Row, row for the night waves rule
A listless adrift in this torpid mind
Onwards to roam and deadly intent
Shivers with the afternoon breeze
And soon the head rests to rock laid
Nobody but own self to linger free
A sunbeam to share my own shadow
Outward bound eyes and drifting dreams
This haste serves nothing but time
Only the final glance serves to inspire.

SEVENTY THREE

These Secrets

There is no travesty in justice
Unless it is you that is deceived
There are no barriers in your freedom
Unless your mind has been stolen
There is no technology invading your space
Unless you're in the CCTV
There is nobody watching you
Unless your ego is bigger than yourself
There are no obstacles to richness
Unless there is a conspiracy
There isn't an alien after you
Unless you're living on Mars
Paranoia, paranoia
It really gets to you
Paranoia, paranoia
It becomes your enemy
Everything of perception
Altered by your reality
Everything there isn't really here
It's actually walking behind you
Your mummy's close friend
An agent of the FBI
Your daddy's wallet
Funded by the FSB
Paranoia, paranoia
It really gets to you
Paranoia, paranoia
Who's knocking on your mind tonight?

SEVENTY FOUR

Love's Moral Fibre

Romance is never dead
It comes in many traits
Call it lust or call it love
We all crave this feeling
Warriors on the battlefield of life
Celebrate with a bout of sex
Loners on a game machine
Fantasies about their ideal mate
Others scurry down back streets
Look for the street walkers hawking
Love comes in many different ways
A beating heart or a thumping grunt
Some take it delicately, others rough
There are those who totally abstain
A sin on the character of life
Builds moral fibre in those of babies
Others like it as it comes openly
Romance has no rules, only respect
Cheating is a dirty game that thrills
Flowers a common expression of affection
Nobody knows where love originates
It is embedded deep within our psyche
A loving and warm feeling
We want to be loved and desired
Even the bearded lady wants to love too
The world cannot thrive without it
Love kills, maims and destroys
But the feelings of love cannot be beaten.

SEVENTY FIVE

Nonsense Hues

The pinks blend into the green
Regenerate as we denigrate
A ray of sunshine burst hope
Violent gamma rays imploding
Sorrow on a seashell abandoned
Pebble used for a wronged cause
Transportation mind bomb
Life on the flipside
Twisted thoughts materialism
Hatred of a conventionalism
Innocence lost under a cloud
Spoiled spoilers on a brand
Speed freaks lose control
Nobody ain't safe anymore
This is the 21st Century
Criminal divergence angst
Slipstream tarmac stolen thunder
A haste in the scurried eats
Ticking gadgets ready to blow
Drill for victory to glimmer
An underworld murkiness
Bacon sniffs prowlers
Nice wheels on the stole
Steady with the lashing blade
A victory belongs to no-one
Four by four and locked
No freeing until time spent
Fingers shifty poking hustle.

SEVENTY SIX

Nightwalker

This lonesome road
At the night of nought
Lost in stupor thoughts
Well lit stranger prowl
Streetlights shadow dance
The jewel of the tarmac
No sense of hurry
Just self and foxes
Roaming past sleepers
Hidden behind curtains
Thoughts stolen from dreams
A giggle of lovers
Flare up tobacco
Shuffle off the damp
A new path to nowhere
Leaving nothing but a past
Footprint ardour recede
Into the shadows once again
Nothing to converse but a mind
Tricks of a trickled utter
Kerbstone curvature bend
Horizon spanned concrete
Sightlines adjusted nowhere
Towards the silence of four
A deadly quiet of still
Then it ticks over soon
Dawn on the way rising
Time for homebound headed.

SEVENTY SEVEN

Chase Your Glory

Come down from your ego
Come bring down your fate
Follow this path of destiny
Only a fool goes nowhere

This chasm is yours forever
Grab with every moment
Time is not for losing
Sorrow is for the grieving

Be bold as you prosper
Lose it all again
Stand pride in your fast
Rebuild and reclaim

Life is a circle
A journey with no ending
Onwards and truly forward
For dreams are this way

Never give up
Never give up when it's cold
Never give up
Never give up when it's hard

Stand with pride and joy
This path is yours forever
Ain't nothing to stop you
Your dreams forever yours.

SEVENTY EIGHT

Angst

Rage
Let it flow
Beseech thee
Angst spittle
Confined
Within you
Rage
An inferno
Bubbling within
Simmer cold
Lash out
Constraint
Rage
Burning inside
Repentation
No haste
Redemption
Flow free
Rage
Seething outlash
Futile peace
Coldness inside
Heart broken
Looking brazen
Rage to flow
Rage an inferno
Rage burning
Rage seething.

SEVENTY NINE

The Lost Motor

Goodbye fine motor
Another wheels leaving
Only I was so sure
We'd tarmac many miles
Your engine assured me
Rolling free on the highway
Longing to see new sights
Forever on the roam
Goodbye fine motor
For you were truly mine
Only now my debts are here
And let you go I must
Wheels turning for dreams
A delight in the carrying
Stripped devoid of us
A longing to be free
Now the time has come
For we to depart
No more churning
Motion on the handbrake
Such a delight you were
Pride of undoubting stint
Goodbye fine motor
For you were truly mine
A loss I feel within
A car with no name
Never forgotten
But just a car.

EIGHTY

Seared Bones

This pain
On the tick tock
Hesitated movement
A shuddering clout
Bone and metal
Collide to meet
I am machine
Devoid of human
Flesh sears metal
Cold burns inside
Time ticks slowly
To heal this pain
Wanting to roam
Babysteps at first
Infantile leaps
Dead man's walk
A shuffle
With no rhythm
Soon feet will bide
To make the stride
Forwards and back
Sideways glance
A crowd to delve
Keeping in stride
Momentary pauses
We'll know for soon
Steps will steadfast
A forwarding to come.

EIGHTY ONE

Haste To Be

This is the seventh of the tenth
Coming up to the eleventh
Time ticks as we motion forward
A scurrying of a roof to come
Then possibly will a home bid
We seek to exit this building
Longing to be freed in haste
Time well spent in healing
A doctrination to stay alive
Then the mainstream will come
The hive and the bustle
To be out amongst the throng
No longer just a number
To be a cog and machine
Systems all set to restart
We plunge to conquer
Faces familiar to acknowledge
Lies that were told to stoop
Hospital times changes
Toiled hours for freedom
And this past will forget
That life is just precious
Keep heads held high
Those who judge only lie
For the truth in own heart
No more demon days
Just this flighty day
Cast out as an individual.

EIGHTY TWO

Canteen Shuffle

They come with shuffling feet
In haste to queue to eat
A morsel choice to dislike
Yet they engorge like obese
No control despite eyes
Fork after knife and spoon
Shifting potatoes to mouth
A quickening in time for seconds
No regard for their waistlines
Soon comes the pudding
Always with generous custard
Sometimes room for more
Plates and bowls disregarded
Without a thought for washing up
Feeding the never hungry
Always on time for meals
Time in-between doesn't count
Just eyes bigger than plates
Waiting and ticking for more
Then with a suddenness
The dining room emptied
Its purpose forgotten and done
No-one gives a damn
To those that toil to prepare
Wolves on the hunger prowl
Everything else doesn't matter
Time ticks in-between naps
Then it all kicks off again.

EIGHTY THREE

Tree

The greenness of scree
A slithering on the bow
Motionless until the wind
Or comes a carefree bird
Spring in the air
A blossom of green
Nature comes to dance
In the first dawn light
Shimmering leaves
All dance to fickle
A blossoming on the go
Regenerate in perpetuity
Another year of growth
Tree rings to record
Standing taller
With all its pollen
Shades of flowers
In the pink and purple
A loving daze
Couples underneath
Initialised bark
Loving memories
Under the trees
Forever a joy
Such trees
Of blossoming days
Underneath trees
A dancing joy.

EIGHTY FOUR

Exit Dreamer

This is the second of the eighth
Time stretched into the distance
So many doctors and nurses skimmed
While treatment woes in measured times
Pray for ticks ahead to be another five
A watchful eye on the keen exit
The walking blues will remain a while
Yet the sights clamour for more feasts
Those days are yet to come soon
Longing for a freedom reign in bed
To hold flesh and sweat through night
With own cloth and divine smells
A kettle on the boil at own time
The chatter in the kitchen shuffles
Those senses are keenly felt
For now the greenery calms
Carrying hopes on the eased wind
To motorise far and find the beach
Smells of the sea and salty lips
The twins of love and amour
Choices to come and no other
Life enriched for this experience
Will it be a lifelong companion
Or shuffling along life's corridor
Loneliness a 20th Century sin
Locking up the immoralised mind
Loving the random steps of life
Towards the keenly felt exit.

EIGHTY FIVE

Inside Indoors

They come in their lonesome ones
An opening of the sealed entrance
For once the door's shut they've got you
As long as you're inside there's no out
Exit is a difficult concept for some
For living is a nightmare to condone
A mind mashed with made up monsters
And eternal torment of the voices
There are those who waste nothing
Knowing that rationale is here
A mind so finely constructed inside
That only external tidiness is the sign
There are those who fear God
Tormented by their own internal demons
A doctor with a mind so fine
Dishes out the magic pills to subside
Everything has an order on the ward
An upset is the latest gossip
Another departure the hottest talk
Nobody ever really leaves
Except those who fight the system
Longing to be free out there
All eyes on the locked exit
For soon a pass will come to open
Then soon out on the streets again
Raging to be part of life
Just don't keep a beady eye
On the ever decreasing clock.

EIGHTY SIX

Keystroke Mantra

With a silent blast
We lifted the great mind
A burrowing into work
Then return cast upon
Open the laptop
And bedevilled by details
Had I really done this
Or have I changed
Work and technology
Information and communication
A burrowed mind unravels
Soon keystrokes return
Sitting uneasy
Exercises on a futility
Smelling in future
The return of the commute
It's exciting to know
How good banality feels
A longing to get out
Haste in the slowing down
Simply one thing to wait
A home for the future
A future to earn for
Writings will return
Payments to be earned
This is a reality checked
Reality kicking in my head
Hurrah to tomorrow.

EIGHTY SEVEN

Lip Service

When dawn rises
So does my heart
For her name is never far
As I long to hold her
Beside me in warmth
Skin to skin
Tightness squeezing
We kiss gently
And ignore the day
For togetherness we crave
And together we stay
Her love is gold
Her lips divine
Nothing out there
Beholds what she has
A blossoming love
Is all we cherish
A blossoming love
Is all we desire
With golden hearts
Until one again
The sun goes down
And only then
Will we kiss some more.

EIGHTY EIGHT

The Cost Of It All

This is the reversed crimson
No negative in my neutrality
A senseless void in the darkness
A platter of multitude mass
Footsteps recede into your shadows
Nobody ever bears witness
A sorrowing on the treason
While wondering if tomorrow will come
Surplus in the profitable loss
Someone's trash is another's silver
Money always on the making
Whereas for other destitute awaits
These streets are not for the caring
Hardcore and attitudes
Life on the constant plunder
We are the new vultures
Nobody left to bury in a pauper's grave
For even being deaf isn't free
Life stood at the roundabout
People nonplussed at this decay
No machine can replicate
This feeling of total despair
For today the birds are not singing
Batteries flat in a hearing aid
Only the sighted know colours
When everybody's really blind
Life is for the churning
A mass of morassed thoughts.

EIGHTY NINE

To Soar High

In the midst of the fallen evening
When birdsong decrees nightfall
A bonding of two spirits
Allowing for lips to meet
Of joy and siren songs
Bringing a blossoming of love
This is life personified
In sensation arousal grows
The future is here right now
All the tomorrows glow assured
Her eyes are pools to dive in
Mane in which fingers dance
She is a golden soul alive
And all the doubts dissipate
As always a hesitate
But that's the challenge of life
Each day brings a different joy
But tears are never heartbroken
In this togetherness we sing
Words not necessary for the dance
Longing and in desire
Togetherness becomes our game
And when darkness falls
We cast aside knowing to meet
There is no barrier for our wait
For this is a loving alive
And her name is in my heart
As I hope mine on hers.

NINETY

She's Out There

Adam and Eve sat in the garden of paradise and ate an apple
Love knew no boundaries afterwards
Let's go find our garden of paradise wherever we go
This land has plenty of beautiful sights
Let's dance together in every fading sunset
Stand in the calm crystal clear seas
I will gently hold your hands
As our flesh comes to meet together
Love is for an eternity
No matter the struggles of life
For with you I can breathe with joy
And together we create life to blossom
May your boys be welcomed and see the joy in their mother's
eyes
Life is for the living and not ending
No more doubting minds to befall me
Let's just hold hands forever
And together create a life of comfort and happiness
With you by my side and I beside you
Anything is possible and nothing impossible
Only everyday we must ensure we kiss.

NINETY ONE

Doctrine Dancer

This is the first of the twelfth
A longing to break free
Freedom days linger fresh
As times past by minutes
The longer the stay becomes
It gets slightly irksome
Others who are ill
Impose their mind games
Ward life is no doctrine
Everyday a different nuance
People with their own quirks
Lifelong habits remain
The smokers passively die
The TV is always on trash
Dinner is never a surprise
Cleaners who forge the times
Schedule in and out everyday
Nobody seems on the mend
Trying days with a glean
A smile goes far sometimes
Violence on the ethnic lines
Always a feminine war
It's the evenings
That bring out the worse
Patients all fed
Waiting for medication
Then it all starts again
Another brand new day.

NINETY TWO

The Kissing

This day
I
Kissed
A
Real lady
Who
Kissed
Me back
I am
Reeled with
Her passion
And
Am
Left wanting
More
In wanton
Greed
For
She kisses
Like
No other
And blimey
I'd
Like more
Now
Everyday
Every infinite
Right now.

Predictable Unknown

Of this day that passeth
A mourning of fading sunshine
Sorrow isn't always in the grieving
A loss felt only at night
For each day that comes
Another bereavement on the passing
Yet counterbalanced by a birth
This endless cycle of life
For what is taken is given
Without barter nor exchange
There are those who live in fear
Lives ordered to the full minute
A sense of hesitation
No knowing of borrowed time
There is no-one to judge
For granted in divine powers
Beyond our grasp of redemption
No-one privileged to know
Those that try to predict
May be the doctors of life
All in the nursing
A healing to linger
For when the shadows come
A passing in unexpected
No-one to know the truth
For beyond eyes shut only know
Live life daily as your last
For tomorrow is another dream.

NINETY FOUR

This Weighty Past

This is the fourth of the twelfth
An expanse of time stretched out
The mind glamours to regain
A control on the inbound return
No-one can say much on this journey
Unless extoiled by weary feet
There is always the longing to go
And yet repelled by nature's time
We mull over words like broken arrows
No aim with composed compunction
This is the terminus disease
A starting point that lived ignored
For where the finishing line remains
Is never reached until exhaled last
The darkness I lived in
A sin of the futile mind
Such deals compromised in sin
Nobody knows of such deeds
Beyond the lines of redemption
Only self worth can reclaim
Burrow deep and find your soul
For such fleshy delights compress
Then look aghast at your past
And with a shrug leave behind
Nobody can carry your story
A strong-willed misled warrior
Returning composed homebound
On the fourth of the twelfth.

NINETY FIVE

Future Famine

Oh futile future
Where are you when all I seek is you
Why are you so elusive when I am so blind
I see that all the tomorrows stretch so far
Into a distance that eyes cannot roll
Oh futile future
Where are you when I hunt high and low
Everywhere in this cell confine I see thee
A travesty of time expurged in haste
When today should by rights be tomorrow
Never cease the chattering voices of the mind
That yesterday is the condemned past
Nor of that I'm living right now is the very future
Of that nonsense that I mythically seek
Oh futile future where are you tonight
This sheathening of the day's end
That brings nightfall to my darkness
Nor will light impenetrate my blind
While I search high and low
In this eternal torment of the tomorrows
That my mind seeks oh indeed desires
Oh futile future where do you lie
I cannot rest for today is of turmoil
Oh come to me and take me away
For this sense of time standing still
I cannot bear as it ticks me by
Oh futile future please do not elude me
For I come to realise after all I am the future.

NINETY SIX

These Forgotten Lies

Of sorrow's seasoned lies
The mourners round the rectangle
A hole hoved of futility
Nobody knows the name
This is a something
That had an entity
Living with eternal dreams
Only to be scooped in dirt
Of the fallen that are forgotten
Even the worldly come to lose
Time conquers all
Unless carved in stone
There is no reason
For doubting the dead
For they are gone
Perished to rotten ash
Disease in the memory
Remembrance on a candle
Forlorn in the winds
Cravings are no more
We seek to honour
Forgetting our misdeeds
For soon we shall join
Bearing cold clammy hands
Tick tock is the big clock
A giant in the skies
Everchanging seasons
And soon all to perish.

NINETY SEVEN

Weekend Romance

Of love's wondrous glory
The weekend in basking delight
Time is of no consequence
Except for check-out time
Love in the blossoming
A delight of antic making
Lips to meet as cuddled
A night long slender
While the river passes by
Such love in the making
Delights on the go slow
Tenderness no boundaries
And flesh comes to sear
Her delight is a gentle
His thrust a noble
For love is in the air again
She is a wonder
He is a roamer
Together history in the make
For theirs is a blossoming love
Knowing nothing but their hearts
Only trueness will prevail
For romance in the everyday
Tenderness in their togetherness
Loving in their touching
While lips crunch to meet
All in their blossoming love.

NINETY EIGHT

Nothing Changes

Time ticks like a stinker
No horoscoped future for today
The papers are for burning
Words of triviality soured
Nobody in a future of greeting
All ears on the plastic glued
Ducks wanton violence for bread
The chips were reconstituted
A glamour for the corner shop closing
Alcohol serves to create inbreeding
There is nothing to be gained
From fucking at three in the photocopy room
Only spawned babies with newsprint rumour
A bench forlorn with redundant workers
The brown paper bags carry their sins
A longing for old addictions resurface
Shaking those newly laid foundations
Nobody knows what tomorrow will bring
Despite the plans as advocated by the psychiatrist
Will it hold together or will the gutter reclaim
A lost leading brain devoured by greed
Then everything was for futility despite the words
Locked up for life the ultimate sentence
And to think that this is a pennant for my crime
In which I destructed my own death
And for what only to regain life without reason
But the sun passes without a murmur
And life continues to challenge in us all.

NINETY NINE

Dirty Cheap

Oh the delight of the morning
Away from the street people
Empty cans and stinking of piss
The sun rose to bring another day
Will the street hawkers move on
To sit in the shade of nowhere
Why can't the streets be hosed clean
Like a fresh Spanish promenade
To think that the thousands
Come and discard their junk
Everyone here for their thrill
We don't enjoy the waste
A life spent chasing money
Everything for a tax man to take
Come for the daylight is safe
Live in fear when darkness falls
The neon lights to catch you
Unaware of those prying eyes
A smell of putrid meat
Restaurants with high prices
A selective that gains entry
Live life like it should
On the very edge of creation
Bones for the pavement
A scurrying crunch of feet
This is London life
Nothing else quite like it.

Hunter Of The Mind

Mantra stark the night falls
Of shadows that befall dreams
Wandering aghast in love's bliss
Wondering how it all will end
Life on the torrent stupor
Glimmerings on a silver edge
Broken in pieces to gather
Will it all ever come together
Only the tomorrow can reveal all
Hunting for quivering arrows
Haste in the season's taste
Looking for sorrow's reasons
We hesitate in doubt
Unsure of when to step again
Will fate befall our destiny
Can things be changed with a twist
Love's stories end in shards
A mirror of one's true heart
Hunters on the ridgeback plough
Stars no longer sent to guide
Switch on the awakenings
For senses alert brings fear
Sweat droplets cools brows
Tastefulness in bruised fruit
Keep hunting for life's reason
Everyday brings a different purpose
Just for once we'll lie down
And coolly make love again.

Ink To Nowhere

A stark in the glaring contrast
Freedom an etching of the mind
We're lost in the roaming thought
As winds cast aspirating seeds
A longing to be nonchalance
Seedless in fruitful thinking
There is no sorrow in sleeping
All the flies continue to mulch
Mothers of the world conspire
Dogs panting on mown grass
Let dogma sleep its poem
All hell cast to lose to seep
Continue to nullify slope
While interruptions break the line
A writer with no inspiration
Nothingness to break free
Not a discarded jail bait
We do not think today
Lost in unreasonable thought
An afternoon on the silence
Looking skywards for rain
While blue skies and sun shine
To consider that tomorrow comes
My own mental tormented room
And once again all aspirations
Are lost in stupor of drink
Only this time it is tea.

Wanton Waste

This is the second of the fourteenth
A passing of the nonchalance void
Nobody comes to knock on the door
To remind us all of the execution
Only there is no death passing today
A loss in a sense of time slipping
Caught up in the day's dramas
We seek purpose in all we do
While trying to deduce reason from it all
Just sometimes it is not wise to think
Only to allow it to roll motion free
Even the outside has its moments to pause
While we stand to gaze and blink
Will sorrow visit today or is it fleeing
All the hives of business prosper
Normality sitting on the window ledge
Passing sights with nonchalance glee
Of this day today will bring love
That feeling of being in joy
Waiting for the three to become two
Then senses will kick in to prosper
Can I hold hand in unison forever
Or will the cultural divide break us
These thoughts roam in random
A sensing of hope in dreams
Only the unravelling of the day
Will reveal what truly beholds
Let's enjoy this second of the fourteenth.

ONE HUNDRED AND THREE

Sleep Sleep

Oh of such glorious mornings
A bright shining sunshine
Just for today
Let's keep the curtains drawn
I'd like to hug you for longer
To kiss sweetly gently those lips of yours
To ignore all ticking time
And allow our flesh to be pulled together
A steamy sense of blossoming love
Sleep longer and allow dreams to linger
While eyes shut dreamily gaze
No more duvet wars
For everything is for the sharing
Yes even hot sweaty bodies too
And love will grow its own sensual
Drawn together by our hearts
Such delights of the mornings
If only everyday could be like this
Sweetness in loving vibes
And soon the time comes to wake
But she demands to know
Where is breakfast Sir?

Skeleton

They say that sins are the harbingers of doom
Not necessarily true for all that commit
Sometimes one's awakening is another's sleeping
A blindness that leads to the broken light
We furrow in our blind path of destiny
Looking for the rumoured reason to exist
The roads really do lead to nowhere
It's the destination in mind that matters
Longing for a heart to be filled with love
When the seasoned path is filled with shards
Broken dreams only come when it is willed
For her heart cannot commit to the love of me
Only time will show the aghast of truths
And who knows what this will bring in collide
The sudden implosion and a mess left to swill
Only the vultures care to eat the remnants
But sometimes when left to prosper in fate
We'll not forecast the brimful storm of mind
For reality knows other than destiny soon to reveal
And once again feet will walk with pride
Leaving a heart filled with joy and another broken
Only for not to know is to live at the edge
Of life's forcibly living energetic reason
Exposed to exist in season's living to ream
For the skies will always float on tearful clouds
And tomorrow will always come no matter what
Just forward with an open heart and mind
Allow life to live without dedication to be free.

Hombre

Here comes the steadiness of the broken hand
A loss in leading the thoughtless ink
No sense of direction despite the man's blindness
For with his ears music becomes devoid
He leads with a green sabre of coldness
A warrior's stride behind the wheeled chariot
His is of senses alternated sensual delight
Only the broken perception of his own to know
Out in the big badlands of London's streets
No shame in the jostling for own's space
Those around are truly the senseless
For no thought nor consideration mollified
He wears black for there are no colours
Only a copyrighted slash of his own to boast
Ladies are an unfamiliar terrain despite eager hands
He has the will but lacks the raconteur's wit
Of such long sweaty delights that are denied
His path is not purely devoid of pleasure
For with a swift hand he can become pissed
In the crowd he becomes the cheerleader
Without the egging on of a cruel crowd
A moth for he is drawn to his own light
Burned by only his own mental limitations
A parachute holds no fear for his courage
For life everyday brings toughness to his skin
Out there and making his own mark
Out there and creating his own journey
The courage of this crazy hombre who smiles.

ONE HUNDRED AND SIX

Flopped

There is no respite in this terminus
A last stop gap of the false waiting
Some of the ether soaked creatures here
Fail to grasp all that life has to offer
It's the offal in the head that gets to them
A seasoning of furrowed slewed thought
Time ticks like it does nowhere else
Only a sense of uneasy consciousness remains
People were troubled by their lopping heads
A shake that does not bring within ease
Another sunset fades into the broken horizon
We long to strive to kick start and breathe
There's nothing except a vast space of time
Longing to scrabble into violent motion
But only to kick away the boredom blues
Only for some of us unfortunate ones
With a trigger happy death switch itching loose
Must find the deviation within inside
To avoid these blues induced destruction hues
Only there's nobody that can see it but their own minds
A lasting lifetime legacy that lasted four seconds
Shorter than a premature ejaculation
And suddenly life is in a doctor's full glare
Oh to think that nine times done over
Hopefully the last and no freedom's roam
No more chances for the impulsive
This is the last path freely chosen
Only today I can't see the forever horizon.

These Shards Of Darkness

Of a sloe's misguided malcontent
The slurring of the biled twisted tongue
A shimmering of the imaginary eye
No hope in this fading summer
Violence took away the grandeur
Of murderous intent without glamour
Soon the cravings shifted elsewhere
And the blue vapours filled the air
A longing to be oblivious cold
With this denial of wronged reality
It soon took a grasp too harsh
And the fall was not long to follow
No matter the greed of alternated
It leads to a downfall
This grasping mantle doesn't relish
No freedom down this track
Needles were never a problem
Only ensuring the cash flowed freely
Then it comes sudden like a crash
And harm began to perish
The fall was broken only by miracle
Of no false witness sighted to know
My own company underneath stars
Soon the loss in faith of humans
Thanks to the birds and the fishes
That came to save this soul
A torture to be broken free
Of addiction's false glamour woes.

This Beating Heart

This is the second of the fifteenth
A realisation of the tenth here
Confined to this juggernaut of the mind
Reason has defied logic to remain
The sun now bolsters its setting down
Another slow evening on the break down
Words warble on the parakeet's wings
A wonder in this southern loaded land
Of time to wonder ahead to forecast
Waiting for bricks and mortar to come
This beating heart awaits a home
For sorrow has beaten its final tune
A last reckoning for the future is defined
Another survival of any fall is futile
They will come with malicious intent
Forever perished behind hidden walls
It has been fifteen years since the last
And now for the hopeful eternity
Waiting for nothing but freedom's roam
A lady on the waiting forever sings
Music is the opium of the everyday
I shall enforce to finish the tune
Let's see what comes of this tenth chance
For nine lives lost is enough now
Onwards with the living perishables
A world in awaiting for adventures
All it takes is footsteps to soldier
Life in its eternal glory manifest.

Hesitation Dreams

Let's travel to the end of this road
A journey filled with calamities
No need to go fishing for thoughts
Freefall thinking only brings fraught
Let the sun bleach your head
Rain to wash away the woes
Life's a-rolling churning nought
Onwards with the spirit of the wind
Ain't nobody going to guide you
No amount of persuasion to distract
Just focus ahead on your soul
For your heart's beating you there
Let this be the last of the death
A woe that's been heavily carried
Freedom a double edged word
Nobody to fetch your dreams
Onwards with the falling star
A night's a pleasure to walk in
The silence gives you awe to inspire
Something to reflect your mind on
This is a path of the lifewalker
Aware of all living subconsciously
All is one and one is all
We grasp everything in spirit
Let this path now transverse
No more influential woes
The final deadbeat journey
Homebound towards my true heart.

Breaking Free

This is the first of the new
A discarding of the past
The fifth day of the fifteenth
A longing to break free
When will the writing end
For the time has come to cry
There are songs that are unloved
Unworthy of its millions imposed
A surreal world I can't get in
But do I want to be there
Instead I'll bide my time
And let it come to me
For writing has its pride
But creativity knows no bounds
Others took their time
Climbing the ivory towers
Sometimes at the top is a fool
With wieldy hands on the money
Control of the new world order
A blindness in profit's sin
I'll be part of the game
Even if fingers get burned
Longing for a laugh
With the beautiful people
For theirs is an illusion
That everybody aspires to
Image is everything
Never mind the heart's woes.

ONE HUNDRED AND ELEVEN

This Surrounding Ego

This is the sixth of the fifteenth
For on the fifth came the breakthrough
Tonight all shall be stripped bare
While the lady drinks firewater
Sister on the financial prowl
A costing of this sublime love
We shall reside grandly
Laid side by side with jowls touching
Will come the night of peace
Or firewater scouring monsters
Love is in flux
Never a steady state of still
This keeps the fires burning
For glory's days and nights
A moment to hesitate
Pausing to reflex in peace
Meeting outcast strangers
From her circle alive
Opinions to be formulated
Drinking to be considered
Will the night survive unscathed
A foreboding of the tomorrow
Head plunges into the challenge
For life must be stripped bare
As tonight will she be naked
Supple flesh to touch fleetingly
Love is a blossoming feeling
All beauty in its manifest.

ONE HUNDRED AND TWELVE

Slipping Apart

Oh maximus delirious
Of such wonderous joy
To walk in her line
Slipstream of love's vapours
Time knew no boundaries
When eyes fell into gaze
A celebration of the gathering
The clan once again reunited
They glamour in their clamour
An adorable gnashing of tongue
How the night fleetingly swam
Stars on the invisible dance
Soon the morning's to come
And gone in the chariot
Towards budgetary palace
Where love will simmer
Through to early risings
A reluctant awakening
But another brand new day
Sitting in the shaded tree
Careless talk and beating hearts
Who wants more of this
When nothing else matters
Then it's time to come part
A whispering goodbye
Shining eyes of joy
Soon time will tick
And we'll reunite again.

Instantly Gone

This is it
Stated the King of Pop
This is it
Stated the deadbeat plop
Life on the churning
Once again on the roll
Forward in motion
No backward glance
Only to know is to go
Wherever the tune calls
A view without curtains
An abode to call home
However short it lasts
Must bloster life's plan
For this is it on the motion
Go and swim in the deluge
For nothing awaits stillness
When feet have to shift
All's changing again
Horizon's cast glances
Outwards scope in hope
Stinking of the ether
Or reeking of smoke
All in the past
Left alone to reckon
For the future is here
A brand new day
Just reminder of the past.

ONE HUNDRED AND FOURTEEN

Perpetual

This mind in perpetual flux
Discontent on the breeding
Restlessness crawls nowhere safe
A faux on the broken dreams
Is this what I strive for
A longing for prosperity
Nobody to know the core
Of this individual in me
I long again to escape
For what is not known
Wondering for so long
And all that remains
Is broken and decayed
A fresh wind blows
I have seen this before
Wanting and in wanton
Is this the home for me
Solo warrior on the prowl
Longing to roam alive
Life is more than this
A cycle of repetition
I long to escape
Sisters on the background hiss
Ladies on the waiting
I cannot stand still
For I must strive haste
Follow or despair
I am only me.

ONE HUNDRED AND FIFTEEN

Breathe

The mind mandrake toils
A lashing of uncertainty
Towards nowhere in my heart
Recoiling like struck fire
I long to be alive
To aghast at attitude
Fuck you is all I wanna say
Beyond redemption woes
A man will smoke if desired
Life on the clean scrapes harsh
Living on the edge where I belong
A frontier of creation's life
Just wanna be free out there
Broken hearts will repair
Eyes need to be refreshed
Breath cleansed once again
Was it just the money
That threw me over the edge
I live in brimstone and fire
Poverty hails me sticky
Out in the wilderness
Just wanting to be free
I walk away for the second time
And shall return for a third
Who's to say no to more
For the town's a dirty whore
Out there to switch off
Out there to find me.

ONE HUNDRED AND SIXTEEN

Reawakening

Is this the flighty mind of indecision
A rashness in the bold enscramble
Longing to go where I belong
Only today I have no home
These footsteps follow my heartbeat
I can only know what surmises
Lost in the stupor of suicidal recovery
A long journey with no end in sight
It takes some forever to find oneself
For others life is a contented entity
Soon I will lose the heart of my love
Watch her disappear over the horizons
I have my own hills to climb
For this is not a sorrowing of ease
Walls all have false summits
Then at the top comes another
The mandrake on this mind
Infernal torment of glee
Longing to be at ease with self
This is the infuriated
When home calls can I cry
For these feet of mine shuffle
Eyes wide awake in want
A cigarette hue and distaste
A view of dawn's rising by the sea
Freedom really a state of mind
The road will soldier on
Here comes the infinite life.

Life Infinity

Oh come for the skies are grey
Bring the jovial blanket of glee
A longing to rejoice in life
For tomorrow sure is another day
We haste to pilfer with content
Filling our empty blanks with goods
A TV does not define life
Only for it does sum up your fears
Is this the real world we occupy
Or an imaginary illusion of yours
There is nothing like standing in wind
A breeze of discontent from the oceans
Listen to the seashore crashing
What are the crunching pebbles
Life is not for the squeamish
A longing to thrive without suffocating
For reasons buried in history
We must stoop backs to sweat
Fake exchange in barter for freedom
I lay down my spade to protest
Toil is not for everyone
Only the feeble come to succumb
Leaders are the people free
Encouraging the future to come home
For now this is the beating heart
Life an eternal journey to pause
Take courage in your stumbling steps
Freedom is for all to share.

ONE HUNDRED AND EIGHTEEN

London's Outcast Cry

Of the mirth that flees my mind
In anguish of the tormented tomorrow
A decision cannot be cast in stone
Until all expletives have been exhausted
For reason struck today with force
And London again opens its arms
I am to stay for sure now
And make my lady a happy one
Without treason any longer
For it cannot be abided internally
Of mind's doubtful corroded steps
While lost in the stupor of expurge
To think there is no reason
When there is every single one
I cannot wait to exchange
This space for another
And soon I shall be gone
For another can have my place
I must become the outcast inside
And recoil at the exuberant
That resides inside me with ink
Penning all that is glory
For nothing else carries untruths
Except the false people with lipstick
And her breasts I relish to grapple
For life today is affirming
I would like to procreate
And restore faith in life.

ONE HUNDRED AND NINETEEN

Return

This is the sixth of the sixteenth
A long slow trial of tribulations
Slow motion bones healing metal
A crunching of this parasite mind
Reality comes knocking and it's too much
Even the buses are speeding today
I long to sit on a bench to observe
But all I have is bare bone in my ass
Wasted muscles seek to return fitness
In time I cannot abide to pass quicker
Of all those who surround me she's there
A constant light even in the daylit skies
Her smile is enough to appeal to my heart
And soon the beating drums of love come
For now I must rein in this restless mind
For it festers festoons in slurriness
Longing to return to the bad old days
But the final suicide prevents all this
A sense of newness returns and longing free
I hesitate to knock on my door of reality
But there it is crashing into my mind
How life springs eternal surprises constant
For not long will the return bring me home
To the place where my heart resides
And love is what keeps me smiling
For without it every day is just grey
But whoa such is the beauty of life
That I have no choice but to persist.

ONE HUNDRED AND TWENTY

Dance To Clouds

Oh wonderous clouds of beyond
How you witnessed this eternal love
A blossoming between two into one
Bringing sunshine smiles into our hearts
Such loving that knows no walls
Only an opening into the future
Loving bliss with beating hearts
Her eyes to swim forever true
While dancing lips preen to prowl
Of joy that is created in the now
Oh this blossoming love indeed true
Such wondrous feelings ever more
She takes me to beyond skies
Love blinds but of such delight
To wrangle into a combine
Of two hearts that become one
Closer we ensheath in true love
For such feelings of eternal delight
Hers is the one I truly desire
A longing to bound forever together
This joy of everyday growing pleasure
Let lips forever explore each other
Yours is truly the one to desire
In bodies that collide to envelope
Longing to roam freely with pleasure
We are two to become one
Forever in our together beating hearts
She is the divine in our blossoming love.